THE UNDEA

VAMPIRES, WEREWOLVES AND ZOMBIES

Jim Pipe

ticktock

THE UNDEAD

VAMPIRES, WEREWOLVES, AND ZOMBIES

North American edition copyright © ticktock Entertainment Ltd 2008
First published in North America in 2008 by ticktock Media Ltd,
2 Orchard Business Centre, North Farm Road, Tunbridge Wells, Kent, TN2 3XF, UK

ticktock project editor: Jo Hanks
ticktock project designer: Sara Greasley
With thanks to: Sally Morgan, Sophie Furse and Elizabeth Wiggans

ISBN 978-1-84696-797 9 pbk

Printed in China

Picture credits (t=top; b=bottom; c=centre; l=left; r=right):
Acclaim Images/Cathy McKinty: 36/37 (main pic). **Amit Gogia CyberMedia Services:** 22bl, 27, 38/39, 42/43 (main pic). **Art Archive:** 83tr. **Bridget McPherson:** 44/45 (main pic). **Chris Harvey:** 12tl. **Colman Lerner Gerardo:** 18bl. **Corbis:** 54/55, 59, 79 (main pic), 70/71. **Demark:** 24tl. **Everett Collection/ Rex Features:** 30bl, 58tl, 66/67 (main pic), 72tl. **FLPA:** 16/17. **Getty:** 14/15 (main pic). **Image Select:** 20tl. **Ioan Nicolae:** 20/21. **Jakez:** 24/25. **Kurt De Bruyn:** 40/41 (main pic). **Magdalena Kucova:** 14bl, 45tr. **Micah May:** 57. **Mindy w.m. Chung:** 40/41 (main pic). **Neo Edmund:** 22/23. **Norma Cornes:** 48/49. **Rex Features:** 28tl. **Robert C. Tussey III:** 48bl. **Ronfromyork:** 18/19. **Shutterstock:** 1, 8bc, 10/11 (main pic), 11tr, 12/13 (main pic), 16tl, 17tr, 24br, 34/35, 42tl, 49cr, 50/51 (main pic), 52bl, 52/53, 54tl, 56bl, 60/61 (main pic), 60bl, 62/63 (main pic), 64/65, 68tl, 69, 70bl, 73, 75, 76b, 80tl, 81, 84/85, 86/87 (main pic), 88tl, 92/93. 92tl. **Steve Truglia (prostunts.net):** 75b. **Superstock:** 76/77 (main pic). **The Kobal Collection:** 66bl, 82/83. **Thomas Grant Readle:** 32/33. **ticktock Media archive:** OFC, 4/5 (main pic), 6/7 (main pic), 6bl, 9, 26bl, 28-29 (main pic), 30-31 (main pic), 33tr, 37tr, 38tl, 46tl, 46/47 (main pic), 47tl, 50tl, 62tl, 71tr, 74bl, 76tl, 78b, 79tr, 80b, 81, 84tl, 85br, 86bl, 89, 90bl, 90/91, 91tl. **Vladimir Pomortzeff:** 32tl. **VTupinamba:** 8tl. **Wendy Kaveney Photography:** 40bl.

VAMPIRES

5

CREATURES OF THE NIGHT

A vampire sinks its long fangs into the neck of its victim—slurp! This evil monster wakes in the night to search for living food. It kills violently and drinks the blood of its victims!

Vampires are dead people who come back to life. During the day, a vampire rests in its grave or coffin. It is active at night, while the rest of the world sleeps.

Beware the vampire! Human blood gives a vampire great strength and supernatural powers. Many vampires can change themselves into a bat, wolf or other night creatures. Anyone bitten by a vampire will become one.

Keep your eyes open! Some vampires do not look like humans. In some parts of the world, they are demons with the body of cats, spiders or polecats.

"I saw the cut had bled a little, and the blood was trickling over my chin. I laid down the razor, turning as I did so half round to look for some sticking plaster. When the Count saw my face, his eyes blazed with a sort of fury, and he suddenly made a grab at my throat."

From *Dracula* (1897) by Bram Stoker.

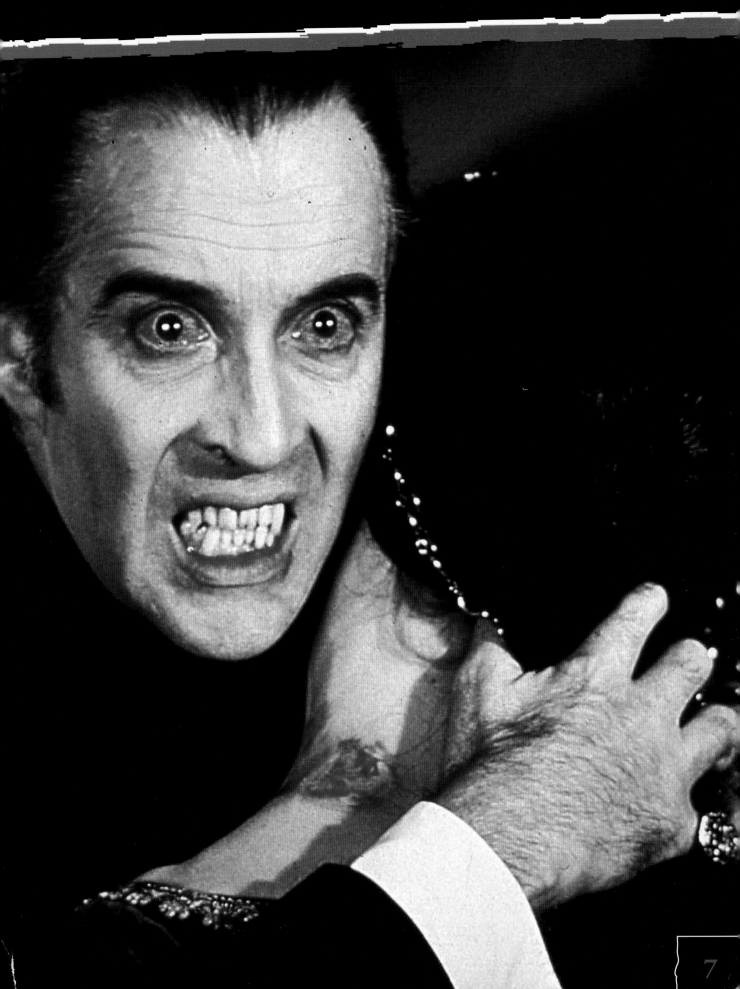

DRESSED TO KILL

If you're on the look out for vampires, watch for long, curling fingernails, pale skin, long white fangs—and really bad breath!

In some reports, a vampire can appear tall and elegant. He dresses in black evening clothes. Often he wears a long cape made from shiny satin that opens out like a bat's wings. Don't be fooled by this smart look. A vampire will quickly turn into a monstrous creature if he's hungry.

Other vampires come in all shapes and sizes. Some dress like you and me. If you're trying to work out if someone is a vampire, don't stare at their cold, glassy eyes for too long. Most vampires can hypnotize their victims. Once in their power, you will be unable to resist!

SHORT, FAT AND DEADLY!

About 200 years ago, vampires in Europe were often short, fat and sweaty! They walked like zombies and smelled gross. Their hideous faces were covered in dirt and their eyes glowed red.

These old-school vampires were happy to slurp down pigs' and cows' blood. They killed their victims by jumping on top of their chests and smothering them. They were messy eaters, too. Their clothes were covered in dried blood.

THE UNDEAD

Vampires can live forever. But their world is cold, dark and lonely. They are afraid of sunlight, so they hide in forests, distant villages and empty castles.

Every part of Europe has its own special vampire. Many vampire sightings come from quiet mountain areas, such as Carpathia and Transylvania in Eastern Europe.

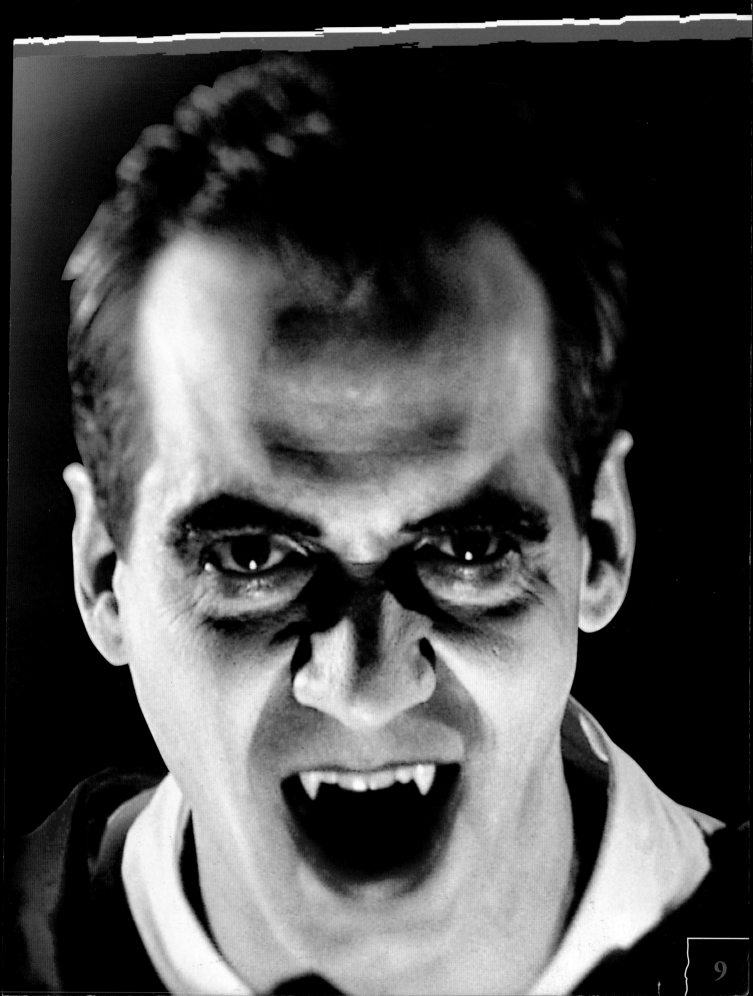

VAMPIRE POWERS

When a human-like appearance is too dangerous, vampires are able to shape-shift. They turn into bats, wolves or even mist.

Life as a vampire is not all fun and games. You must keep killing in order to survive. Without human blood, your body will crumble to dust. Most humans aren't crazy about your nasty bloodsucking habits. Annoying hunters are always chasing after you with a wooden stake.

Luckily for you, vampires have a wide range of supernatural powers to help them in their battle against the living:

- **Strength**—vampires get even stronger as they age.
- **Speed**—they're so fast that human eyes sometimes cannot see them.
- **Agility**—they can climb walls like a lizard.
- **Transformation**—they can turn into bats, wolves, moths, cats, bugs, or rats.
- **Hypnosis**—vampires use this to control their victims.

BEWARE THE GREEN MIST

In some legends, vampires have great power over nature. They can control wind and rain. They can also make great swarms of rats or creepy crawlies attack their enemies.

In Bram Stoker's story, Dracula turns into a green mist to escape vampire hunters. He then enters the houses of his victims by slipping under the door.

VAMPIRE HABITS

Would you like to avoid vampires? A vampire has amazing powers, and he has weaknesses. Learn a vampire's habits and one day it could help you to get away from those nasty fangs!

"The Count grasped my hand with a strength which made me wince... it [the hand] seemed cold as ice, more like the hand of a dead than a living man.

"... his nails were long and fine, and cut to a sharp point... he used one of them to open a wound on his chest, letting his own blood flow..."

A description of Count Dracula from *Dracula* (1897) by Bram Stoker.

During the day, you are pretty safe from vampires. They hate light. Direct sunlight can burn or kill them. Even at night, they prefer rooms lit with candles.

Vampires sleep during the day when they have to be safe in their grave before sunrise. They also have to sleep surrounded by dirt from their home country. If a vampire travels abroad, he brings along a coffin filled with dirt from his home.

If you are escaping from a vampire, remember that he cannot cross running water. Also, in some legends, a vampire cannot enter a house unless he or she is invited in.

BACK OFF, BLOODSUCKER!

Have bat-like creatures been flapping at your window? Do you hear strange howling noises outside? Is there any green mist rolling across your yard?

If you think a vampire is after you, don't worry. There are ways to get rid of it. Place bulbs of garlic near windows and doors, and around your neck. When close to a vampire, a crucifix or a bottle of holy water will make it back off. Vampires also stay away from crosses as they are an ancient symbol of goodness. Some vampires even hate the sound of ringing bells.

Children in Malaysia once wore a black silk armband to protect themselves from a vampire called the bajang. The Roma gypsies believed that socks stolen from a dead person are a powerful (but smelly) way to keep vampires away!

OUT FOR THE COUNT

It might surprise you to know that vampires are very fussy! You can use this fact to save yourself. In Serbia people leave a pile of poppy seeds near a vampire's grave.

When it rises from its grave the vampire won't be able to walk past without counting the seeds. (This is not the reason why Dracula is called "Count"!). A big enough pile will keep a vampire busy all night.

VAMPIRE HUNTER

A vampire hunter's task is not an easy one. Finding a vampire is tough enough. Then you have to kill it—before it kills you. Top tip: hunt it during the day while it sleeps!

Where should you start looking? The countries with most vampire reports include Serbia, Greece and Transylvania in Europe. Once you get there, look for local vampire activity. Signs that a vampire is on the prowl include mysterious deaths, visits from a dead neighbor and messed-up graves.

Okay, you find the signs you were looking for. Now lead a horse around the graveyard or old castle where you think the vampire has its coffin. The horse will get spooked when it gets close. When you dig up the corpse, look for blood around the mouth, long, talon-like fingernails and fangs.

Last, but not least, kill the vampire! A wooden stake through the heart is the best method. Then cut off its head and burn the body. This way there's no chance of the vampire coming back to life.

TOOLS OF THE TRADE

If you fight a vampire, the following tools are useful:

- Wooden stakes— well sharpened!
- Mallet—to bash stakes into a vampire.
- Mirror—if you can't see a person's reflection, they're a vampire!
- Cross/crucifix—to keep the vampire at bay.
- Garlic—to protect your own neck.
- Saw—to cut off their head.
- Crowbar—to open coffins.

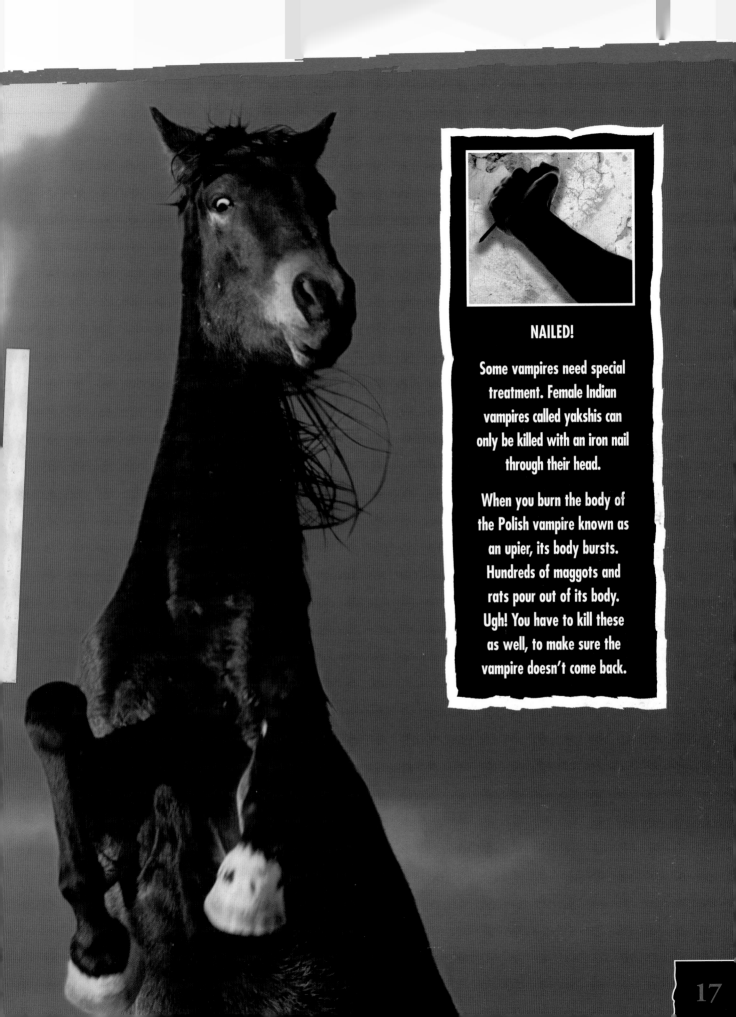

NAILED!

Some vampires need special treatment. Female Indian vampires called yakshis can only be killed with an iron nail through their head.

When you burn the body of the Polish vampire known as an upier, its body bursts. Hundreds of maggots and rats pour out of its body. Ugh! You have to kill these as well, to make sure the vampire doesn't come back.

VAMPIRE SCARES

The man came to a crossroads. It was getting dark, and he was lost. Out of the gloom crept a shriveled creature with a body as white as snow. Suddenly, it pounced. The last thing the man saw was the death's-head tattoo on the monster's face…

This Aztec vampire, known as a civitateo, was spotted in 14th-century Mexico. The civitateo had magic powers which it used to kill travelers.

In fact, people have reported vampire attacks all over the world for thousands of years. But nothing can compare to the wave of vampire stories that swept across Eastern Europe in the 18th century. Terrified villagers took matters into their own hands. They began digging up bodies and burning them. In some areas, angry mobs went on a mad vampire hunt, killing hundreds of innocent people.

THE FIRST "VAMPIRE"

In 1725, the word "vampire" was first used in an official report about Peter Plogojowitz. A week after his burial, in the Serbian village of Kisilova, other villagers started dying from a mysterious illness.

The surviving villagers were convinced that Peter had turned into a vampire. They dug up his body and thrust a sharp stake through his heart before he could kill anyone else.

THE BLOODY COUNTESS

Erzsebet Bathory (1560–1614) was a Hungarian countess. Erzsebet thought that taking a bath in the blood of girls would keep her young and beautiful. So, her servants tricked girls into Erzsebet's castle, where they were murdered.

The truth came out when local people became suspicious about the missing girls. In 1610, the countess was locked up in her bedroom and fed through a tiny slot in the wall. She died four years later.

LIVING VAMPIRES

On St Bartholemew's Day, 1469, Prince Vlad Dracula had 30,000 men stuck on spikes. The prince then set up a picnic table and ate lunch surrounded by this forest of corpses.

The word vampire is sometimes used to describe people who commit terrible, bloody crimes. The best example is Vlad Dracula (1431–1476). He ruled a part of Romania in Europe called Wallachia from this huge castle.

Vlad was known for his cruelty. His second name, "Dracul," means dragon or devil in Romanian. He was famous for sticking his enemies on wooden spikes, giving him another name—Vlad the Impaler. Bram Stoker partly based his character, Dracula, on the Impaler.

Vlad's cruelty struck fear into both his own people and his enemies. In one story, two ambassadors from a nearby kingdom refused to take off their hats during a visit to Vlad's castle. The prince ordered that the hats be nailed to their heads, so that the men should never have to remove them again.

WORLD OF VAMPIRES

Vampire hunters, brace yourself. If you think Dracula is trouble, just wait until you bump into one of these strange yet terrifying vampires from around the world!

- **Lagaroo:** Found on the Caribbean island of Grenada. This vampire looks like a sweet old lady during the day. Don't be fooled— at night it sheds its skin to become a flying ball of flame.

- **Kuangshi:** This giant vampire from China has glaring red eyes, sharp fangs and talons, and is covered in a thick coat of green hair!

- **Churel:** From India, this female vampire has a black tongue and back-to-front feet. She especially enjoys munching on young men.

- **Asanbosam:** This vampire lives deep in the forests of West Africa. It looks like a human, but has hooks on its legs and iron teeth. It dangles from a tree and scoops up its victims from the ground as they walk by.

- **Manananggal:** This winged vampire from the Philippines does a neat trick. The top half of her body separates from the bottom half!

MALAYSIAN MAYHEM

Malaysia is home to some nasty vampires. The bajang is a demon vampire that looks like a polecat. Some sorcerers keep it caged in a bamboo jar and feed it eggs and milk. They use the bajang against their enemies—the victims die from a mystery illness after being bitten.

Another Malaysian vampire, the penanggalan, looks like a woman during the day, but at night its head comes off. It flies around with parts of its stomach hanging out from the back of its neck!

23

UNUSUAL BLOODSUCKERS

You hear a growl coming from the kitchen. Inside, a strange-looking fruit is rolling around the floor, leaving traces of blood. Don't worry, it's only a vampire pumpkin!

In Bosnian folklore, watermelons and pumpkins kept for more than 10 days after Christmas can turn into vampires. Luckily, these monsters aren't very dangerous as they have no teeth. However, they are not the only bloodsucking plants. In the movie, *Little Shop of Horrors* (1986), a worker at a flower shop grows a meat-eating monster plant. It begins murdering people to feed its blood hunger.

Vampires can take on many other strange forms, such as bugs, chairs, houses, and plants. There are tales of vampire cars, motorcycles, and ships.

LITTLE SUCKERS

In Malaysian folklore, the pontianak is a child vampire. It cries like a baby to trick its victim into coming closer. Then it digs into the victim's stomach with its long, sharp fingernails.

In Serbia, the human children of vampires were known as dhampirs. These children had the power to find and destroy their invisible vampire relatives.

REAL-LIFE VAMPIRES

Some vampire stories are based on real bloodsuckers. For example, vampire bats really exist.

They live in South America and feed on sleeping pigs, horses, and, very rarely, people! They bite a soft part of the skin then lap up the blood with their tongue.

DRACULA, LORD OF DARKNESS

DRACULA! The name alone sends a chill down the spine. Irish writer Bram Stoker did not make up the idea of vampires. His character Dracula is still the most famous vampire in the world.

In Bram Stoker's book, Dracula lives in a far away castle in Transylvania. He moves to London, England where there are many victims to feed on. He travels by ship, in boxes filled with dirt from his homeland. The dirt keeps him alive. Once in England, Dracula attacks young women and turns them into vampires. He uses these vampiresses to protect him.

Vampire hunter, Dr Van Helsing, and a group of friends fight Dracula using garlic and crucifixes. They force him back to Transylvania where he is killed by a knife through the heart.

Bram Stoker dreamt up new powers for vampires. His Dracula could climb walls and turn into mist. He could also walk about in daylight, without turning to dust. It is also from Stoker's book that we get the idea that vampires cannot be seen in a mirror because they do not have a soul.

VAMPIRE RESEARCH

Bram Stoker took his ideas from many places. The female vampires in his story may be based on sídhe (pronounced shee), bloodsucking monsters from Irish myths. The technology used by the heroes was brand new when Stoker was writing. So, the heroes chase Dracula across Europe on steamships and trains, and track him using a telegraph.

"The victim is never bled to the point of death... is helped to develop the vampire senses... is taught to kill, to search for a coffin, to travel across the world without raising suspicion, is taught how to live a wealthy life in the manner of a grand lord or lady..."

Here an experienced vampire explains how to train a victim in the ways of the vampire. From *Interview with the Vampire* (1976) by Anne Rice.

VAMPIRE NOVELS

If you were going to write a vampire story, what would your vampire be like? An old-fashioned vampire like Dracula living in a gloomy castle? Or a modern vampire living in a big city?

Bram Stoker is just one of hundreds of writers who have written about vampires. The first vampire books were written during the vampire hunts of the 18th century. They read like science reports. The most famous was written by a French monk, Dom Augustin Calmet, in 1746. Calmet really believed in bloodsucking vampires. But he couldn't explain how they came to be alive.

The English poet, Lord Byron, started a story about vampires. This book, *The Vampyre: A Tale* (1819), started a new vampire craze. It featured many new ideas about vampires. It was the first book to show them as tall aristocrats. In old folk tales they were always stupid monsters. Thirty years later the spine-chilling *Varney the Vampire* (1847) was so popular it went on for 220 chapters and 868 pages!

MOVIE AND TV VAMPIRES

"**I**n every generation there is a Chosen One. She alone will stand against the vampires, the demons and the forces of darkness. She is the Slayer." From *Buffy the Vampire Slayer* (1997).

Vampire stories are very popular. Many recent movies mix new ideas with old ones. In the TV show, *Buffy the Vampire Slayer*, Buffy Summers is chosen to battle against vampires and other supernatural demons. Set in modern California, Buffy's town of Sunnydale sits above a Hellmouth. This is a gateway for demons to enter the world of the living. Buffy is a high-kicking martial arts expert, but she still uses an old-fashioned stake to kill vampires.

Many vampire movies focus on the vampire hunter. In *Van Helsing* (2004), the hero fights against flying vampires and other nasty monsters. In *The Fearless Vampire Killers* (1967), two useless vampire hunters struggle against a horde of bloodsuckers. At a ball, they look in a mirror and see only themselves—everyone else in the room is a vampire!

REWRITING FOLKLORE

Movies are constantly rewriting the old vampire stories. In *Blade* (1998), the hero is half-human, half-vampire. This is because his human mother was bitten by a vampire while she was pregnant. The vampires in *Blade* are recognized by their tattoos. These show which family of vampires they belong to.

Some movies, such as *The Lost Boys* (1987), feature good vampires that try to be human. They fight against their thirst for blood. The vampire hunters in this movie are two teenage boys who suspect their mother's new boyfriend is a bad vampire.

WAKING THE DEAD

In the past, many people believed that vampires caused plagues. A plague is a large outbreak of a deadly disease. Between 1347–49 the Black Death wiped out almost a third of people living in Europe.

With so many people dying, some may have been buried alive by mistake. So, when their coffins were opened, these bodies would seem fresher. The plague gave them white skin and red gums— just like vampires!

DO VAMPIRES EXIST?

"The coffin was covered in blood. Fresh blood flowed from the dead man's eyes, nose, mouth and ears. Fresh nails grew from his fingers and toes. When the villagers plunged a stake into its heart, the corpse groaned!"

This report was written in 1727. It tells how Serbian villagers dug up the body of Arnold Paole. Local people believed that he rose from his grave to kill four villagers and suck the blood of their cattle! But was this man really a vampire?

No one caught Paole sinking his teeth into a victim. The blood in the coffin was probably a mix of the reddish liquid produced by a rotting body, and blood that naturally becomes runny again after death. It is also common for people's nails and hair to grow after they die. The groan was probably caused by gases escaping from the rotting body when the stake burst it open.

Perhaps the most simple explanation is that when people started dying mysteriously in the village, it was easiest to blame someone who was already dead!

VAMPIRE DISEASES

Vampires may have been people suffering from rare diseases such as porphyria. Sufferers are so sensitive to sunlight they can get sunburn on a cloudy day.

Not surprisingly, they spend most of the time hidden in dark places—like a vampire! Porphyria can also make teeth and fingernails turn red, making them look bloody.

WEREWOLVES

BEWARE THE FULL MOON!

A **full moon lights up the night sky. OWWWHHH! A howl fills the air. It strikes fear into the bravest heart. Watch out! A werewolf is on the hunt for human flesh!**

A werewolf is a man or woman who turns into a wolf when there is a full moon. By night, a werewolf is a savage monster. It kills and eats anyone or anything it meets. By day, it is human again.

If you're lucky, the only werewolves you'll see are in movies and books. But hundreds of people say real werewolves have attacked them!

Werewolves are feared all over the world. In South America, a wolfman called a lobizón eats babies and animal dung. In Germany, boxenwolves hunt for horses to eat.

Do these terrifying monsters really exist? Read on and decide for yourself...

WOLFMAN

The word "were" means "man" in Old English. So a werewolf means a "manwolf."

Some werewolf stories are thousands of years old. European werewolf legends feature witches who can turn themselves into wolves. In other parts of the world, witches change into night hunters such as were-bears, were-foxes and were-leopards.

FROM MAN TO WOLF

Bones crack, muscles grow. A giant jaw with long fangs bursts from his mouth. Thick, dark hair sprouts all over his body. Claws spring from his toes and fingers. Man has become wolf!

It's not all fun being a werewolf! Okay, so you become bigger, faster, and stronger. But changing from a man into a monster really hurts!

In some reports, werewolves look half-wolf, half-human. In early Native American legends, wolfmen walked on all fours. In later legends, they began walking upright to become more human. Many of the wolfmen seen in Europe also walk on two legs.

In other stories, werewolves are more like giant wolves. They run on all fours. Their bodies are covered in silver fur. Their red eyes glow like burning coals in the dark.

"Niceros tells of a friend who stripped off his clothes and hailed (howled at) the stars... all at once he became a wolf... Niceros heard that a wolf had been worrying cattle and had been wounded in the neck. On his return home, he (Niceros) found his friend bleeding at the neck, and he knew that his friend was a werewolf..."

From *Satyricon,* a book by a Roman writer called Petronius, written about 2,000 years ago.

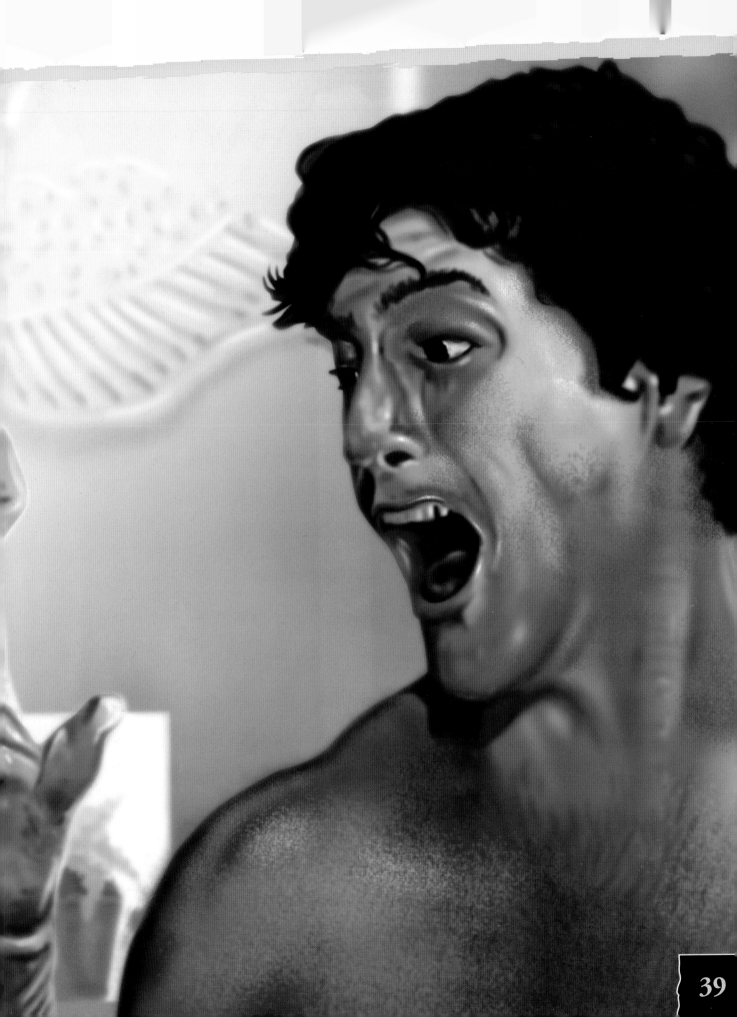

THE CURSE OF THE WEREWOLF

You wake up in a field, miles from home. Your clothes are torn. There is blood all over your hands and face. You have a terrible headache and you can't remember anything from the night before. Hmmm… sounds like you're a werewolf!

Do you want to be a werewolf? The smart answer is no!
So, you need to avoid:

- Being bitten or scratched by another werewolf.
- Eating the flesh or brains of a wolf.
- Drinking water from a wolf's paw print.
- Swimming in a cursed stream (in Greece).
- Being born on Christmas Eve (in Italy).

Actually, most people cursed with being a werewolf don't like it.
They feel terrible about killing other people. But they can't help it.
Some werewolves try to kill themselves to be rid of this curse.
Watch out, though. A few do enjoy having the superhuman strength and speed of a werewolf. They also love the taste of human flesh!

WOLF MAGIC

German werewolves are called boxenwolves. They change into wolves by putting a magic strap around their body. Horses are their favorite food. In one German village, a man was paid to whisper magic words into the ears of horses each night. The words protected the horses against the boxenwolves.

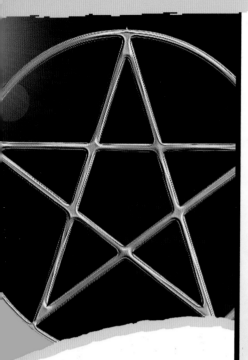

HOW TO SPOT A WEREWOLF

Do your friends have...
a) rough hair on their palms?
b) an extra long index finger?
c) really thick eyebrows that meet in the middle?

TELL-TALE SIGNS

Some werewolves have tattoos of the moon on their body. Others are marked with a pentagram. This five-point star is an ancient magic symbol. A werewolf may see a shadow of this star on the forehead of its next victim.

Russian werewolves have hair under their tongue. They also have blood-red fingernails and a small tail hidden under their clothes!

If so, they might be a werewolf! There are other ways to spot a werewolf. Werewolves have very bad breath and terrible body odor! Some werewolves are even said to have purple urine.

A werewolf's habits can give it away. Many werewolves avoid running water, such as rivers and streams. Werewolves also hate light. In some legends they can't even look up at the sky.

Are your neighbors always replacing their pets? It may be a sign that they are eating them. When there's a full moon, you may also be kept awake by howling from next door.

Finally, watch out for someone who hangs around graveyards. They may be a werewolf looking for freshly buried bodies to munch on.

KILLING A WEREWOLF

The werewolf snarled as it backed into the corner. The hunter aimed his pistol. A single bullet sped from the gun, through the heart of the monster. The werewolf was dead.

In old movies, only a silver bullet can kill a werewolf. In 1767, the "Beast of Gévaudan" (a French werewolf) was shot and killed with a silver bullet made from a holy cup.

However, any weapon that kills a normal wolf will also kill a werewolf. So shotguns, spears, traps, or poison will all work. In the 17th century, the Catholic Church preferred two methods. The first was to cut off the werewolf's head with a double-edged sword. The second was to stab it between the eyebrows with a pitchfork!

Once your werewolf is dead, cut off its head, burn the body and scatter the ashes. Now the werewolf's curse is broken. That means anyone once bitten by this werewolf becomes human again.

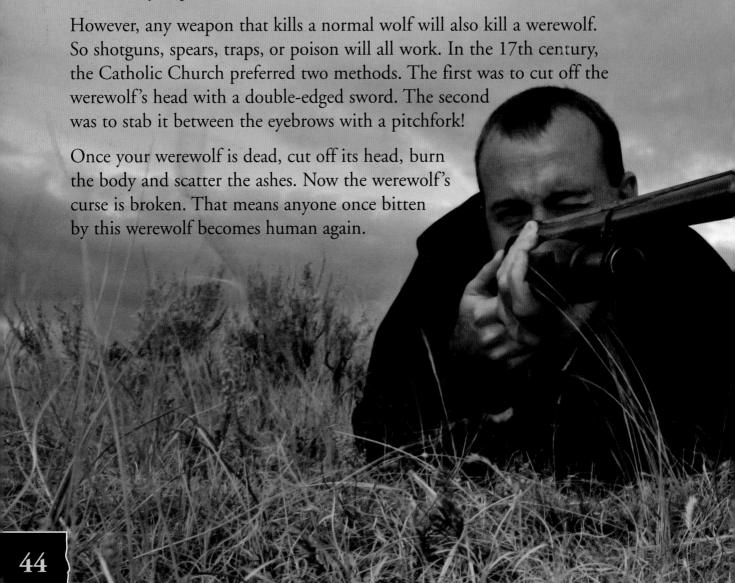

WANT TO BE A WEREWOLF HUNTER?

Are you nuts? Finding a werewolf before it changes is hard. During the day, it behaves like everyone else. It has the brains of a human, so traps won't fool it.

If you find a werewolf after it's changed, try to hurt it. A wound will show up when it turns back into a human. In its human form a werewolf is weaker. Be warned, some werewolves hunt in packs. Help!

"They were like wolves, but their faces were small and long... and they had great ears. The skin on their spine looked like that of a pig. In some villages they ate more than 100 people... These monsters entered houses... they climbed in the night onto terraces, and stole children from their beds."

Werewolves in Iraq described by the writer Denys of Tell-Mahre, around 770 BCE.

THE FIRST WEREWOLVES

A man walks to the edge of a lake. He hangs his clothes on a tree, and then plunges into the water. When he appears on the far side of the lake, he is a wolf!

Members of a secret religion in Arcadia, ancient Greece, believed that jumping into a lake would change them into a wolf. They could only become human again if they had not eaten human flesh for nine years. In 400 CE, a member of this group, Damarchus, won a boxing match at the Olympics. It is said he changed into a wolf during the fight.

Werewolves are as old as story telling. The *Epic of Gilgamesh*, written four thousand years ago, features Enkidu. He is a werewolf-like hairy man.

In an ancient Greek myth, King Lycaon of Arcadia chops up his grandson. Then he serves the body to the god Zeus. When Zeus finds out, he punishes Lycaon, by turning him into a werewolf.

A CURSED TOWN

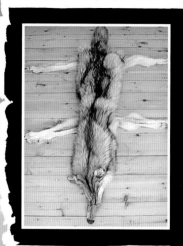

There are many werewolf tales from the Middle Ages. In the 12th century, historian Gerald of Cambridge tells of an Irish priest who meets a talking wolf.

The wolf begs the priest to visit his dying wolf wife. The wolf tells the priest that St Natalis has cursed the town of Ossory, in Ireland. Every seven years, two people from the town must put on wolf skins and turn into werewolves. When the priest visits the dying she-wolf, she peels off her fur. Underneath is the skin of an old woman.

THE GREAT WEREWOLF HUNTS

It is 1439. One summer's evening, a pack of hungry wolves runs silently though the streets of Paris, France. In a single night, they kill and eat 14 people.

In the Middle Ages, people saw wolves as evil killers. In 1300, the town of Vicenza in Italy built new walls as protection against werewolves! In Germany and Serbia, anyone found guilty of being a werewolf had their head cut off and their body burnt.

In Europe, the Catholic Church spread the idea that witches could turn into wolves. Many people believed it was true. From 1520 to 1630, around 30,000 people were killed for being werewolves. They were accused of stealing cattle and killing children. Many people admitted to being werewolves after being horribly tortured.

In Italy, people believed that werewolves grew thick hair inside their skin. Several suspects died after being cut open by doctors.

BUCKLES, BELTS AND BULLETS

In the year 1640, in the town of Griefswald, Germany, many people were dying. It was thought that werewolves were responsible. A group of students decided to take action. They melted down silver buckles to make strong silver bullets. With these bullets, the students were able to shoot the werewolves.

THE BEAST OF GÉVAUDAN

On the night of January 15, 1765, a man struggles through the snow, looking for his son. He sees a shape on the ground. Coming closer, he gasps in horror at the bloody body lying on the ground…

The man, Pierre Châteauneuf, brought his son's body home and sank into a chair. He claimed that he looked up and saw a werewolf's glassy eyes staring at him through the window. Grabbing his musket, Pierre fired at the monster. But it ran off.

This werewolf became known as the "Beast of Gévaudan." People said it had thick, dark hair and an evil smell. In three years, the beast killed over 60 people in the mountains of south-central France. Whole villages were deserted as people fled in terror.

MONSTER OR MYTH?

Several hundred men finally hunted down the Beast of Gévaudan. It was shot with a silver bullet through the heart.

There were rumors that the actual beast was too horrible to show in public. So, the body of a large wolf was carried through the streets.

But was the beast really a werewolf, or just a wolf?

WERE-CREATURES

Abeautiful woman walks into the room. But something isn't right. Is that a tail hidden under her clothing? You happen to see her reflection in a mirror— she's a were-fox!

Humans that turn into beasts are in stories from all over the world. In Indian folklore, people change into were-tigers and were-foxes. In Russia they become were-bears, in Peru were-jaguars. In Chile there are witches who turn into chonchons, a mix of vulture, lion and human.

The Santu sakai are were-monsters from Malaysia, called "mouth men." They have large fangs and love the taste of human flesh. These monsters attack remote villages, killing and eating their victims.

The Berber peoples of Morocco believe in boudas—sorcerers that turn into hyenas. Real hyenas can make a sound just like a human voice. So are these were-monsters all in the mind?

WERE-FOXES

Were-foxes are very popular in the legends of China and Japan. Unlike werewolves, they do not start out as humans. In China, a fox that lived for 500 hundred years could change into a human!

The Japanese were-fox, called a kitsune, is usually female. Its bushy tail can be seen, even when it's in human form. A kitsune turns back into a fox at night. It plays tricks on people.

SHAPE-SHIFTERS

A medicine man dances and chants to the rhythm of a drum. The drum beats faster. The man goes into a trance. He calls out to the spirits, "Now I am an eagle upon your winds, soaring high into the clouds!"

In many cultures there are stories of gods and people changing into animals. This power is known as shape-shifting.

The Navajo Native American people of the southwestern United States tell stories about "skin-walkers." A skin-walker is a healer who uses magic to change into an animal such as a wolf, bear, or eagle.

In Iceland, a hamrammr is a were-creature that changes into the animal it has just eaten. Its strength increases with each animal it gobbles up.

In Mexican folklore, the nahual are witches who turn into wolves, jaguars or eagles. They do this to attack their enemies. The nahual do not like blades, scissors, piles of gray ash, or garlic.

BIG, BAD WOLF?

Native Americans have always looked kindly on "Brother Wolf." They respect a wolf's hunting and tracking skills.

A wolf provides food for all its family, including the old and sick members of the pack.

Wolves once followed the herds of bison that moved across the Great Plains of North America, just like the Native American hunters.

FAMOUS WEREWOLF STORIES

Two Viking warriors come across a hut deep in a forest. Inside are two wolf skins. When Sigmund and Sinfjotli (the warriors) put on the skins, they cannot take them off. Now they are werewolves.

These werewolves appear in the *Volsunga* saga, written in 1300 CE. In the story, the Vikings agree that if one of them fights more than seven men, he must howl for help. Sigmund learns that Sinfjotli has fought 11 men without howling for his help. He is so angry he attacks and wounds Sinfjotli. However, he looks after him until their curse is broken.

Werewolf stories were also popular in the 19th century. *Wagner the Wehr Wolf* was written by G. W. M. Roberts in the 1840s. It tells how a German man sells his soul to the Devil. He can live forever, but has to become a werewolf every seven years.

In *Dr Jekyll and Mr Hyde* (1886) by R. L. Stevenson, a scientist creates a drug that turns him into a murdering beast. Eventually he begs a friend to kill him so he can't harm anyone else.

"He put the glass to his lips and drank at one gulp. A cry followed; he reeled, staggered, clutched at the table and held on... his face became suddenly black and the features seemed to melt and alter."

From *Dr Jekyll and Mr Hyde* by Robert Louis Stevenson (1886). This scene describes how the scientist Dr Jekyll turns into the savage Mr Hyde.

MOVIE WEREWOLVES

"**E**ven he who is pure in heart, And says his prayers by night, Can become the wolf when the wolfbane blooms, And the moon is full and bright." (Ancient rhyme, used in the movie *The Wolf Man* in 1941).

Werewolves have been scaring moviegoers for almost 100 years. In 1913, the silent movie *The Werewolf* used a real wolf as a werewolf! Later movies, such as *The Wolf Man* (1941), used an actor with hairy make-up. In recent movies, such as *Van Helsing* (2004) and *Brotherhood of the Wolf* (2003), the werewolves were created by computer graphics.

In the TV series, *Buffy the Vampire Slayer*, Buffy's friend Oz is a werewolf. When he is about to turn into werewolf, he gets his friends to lock him up. If they don't have time, they shoot him with a drug. Then Oz sleeps off his rage.

In *Teen Wolf* (1985), Michael J. Fox plays a teenager who uses his wolf powers to become the star player on the basketball team!

ANIMAL PEOPLE

There are many movies with were-creatures. In *Cat People* (1942), a beautiful woman turns into a black panther. In *The Fly* (1958), a scientist turns into a giant fly after an experiment goes horribly wrong.

Comic book characters can also take on the powers of an animal. In the movie *X-Men* (2000), Wolverine is a wolf-like superhero with sharp metal claws between his knuckles.

FACT OR FICTION?

WOLF WORSHIP

Where do werewolf stories come from? In the past, many warriors wore animal skins because they believed the skins would turn them into good fighters. Wearing skins also made them look like scary monsters!

In medieval Germany, people believed that great warriors became wolves when they died. Boys were called Wolfbrand and Wolfgang to make them strong and brave, like a wolf.

Viking warriors called Berserkers wore bearskin shirts. They believed the shirts would make them fierce and strong like a bear.

Before a battle, the Berserkers prayed to the Viking war god, Odin. Then they worked themselves into a fury. The warriors then charged into the fight, howling like animals. No wonder people thought they were being attacked by were-bears!

THE LEOPARD MEN

The Leopard Men were a secret society in West Africa. Local chiefs paid them to kill their enemies. They believed a magic drink made from their victim's stomach turned them into leopards.

A Leopard Man wore the skin of a leopard and an iron bracelet fitted with dangling knives. When he clenched his fist, the knives became claws.

RARE DISEASES?

Some werewolves may be people with a condition known as hypertrichosis. This makes you really hairy.

Another rare disease, porphyria, also makes people look like a werewolf. Their skin changes color, thick hair grows on their face and they become sensitive to light.

DO WEREWOLVES EXIST?

It is 30,000 BCE. In a dark cave lit only by torches, a caveman dabs red color on the wall. He grunts happily. He has painted two-legged human figures—with animal heads!

People have reported sightings of werewolves for thousands of years. But do they really exist? One explanation for the sightings might be the disease rabies. People bitten by an animal with rabies, may act like a wolf and become wild and froth at the mouth.

Most werewolves are probably people with a mental illness. In 540 BCE, King Nebuchadnezzar of Babylon went mad for four years. He thought he was a wolf and let his hair grow wild. Some forms of madness can make people violent or very strong.

During the 16th century, most people who admitted they were werewolves had been tortured into it. People accused others of being a werewolf because they didn't want to be accused themselves!

ZOMBIES

WHAT IS A ZOMBIE?

Y ou hear moans, then shuffling feet. CRASH! An arm grabs at you through the window. CRUNCH! The door crashes in. Zombies are on the hunt for your tasty, tasty brains!

A zombie is a dead person that has been brought back to life. It wanders about with its eyes staring straight ahead and its mouth wide open.

Zombies feed on humans. They love feasting on human brains. They often attack in big groups, ripping people into tiny pieces!

Zombies look like sleep-walking morons, but they are strong enough to rip your body in half, or tear off your head.

The smallest scratch or bite from a zombie can turn you into one, too!

THE FIRST ZOMBIES

Zombies first appeared in voodoo stories from Haiti, an island in the Caribbean. Voodoo is a religion from Africa. It came to Haiti in the 18th century, when people captured in Africa were taken to Haiti to work on farms as slaves.

Reports from Haiti describe the dead being brought back to life by voodoo sorcerers.

TOXIC ZOMBIES

In the last 30 years, a new breed of zombies has appeared—toxic zombies! These creatures have rotting bodies covered in wriggling maggots.

Toxic means poisonous. Toxic zombies come to life when radiation or poisonous chemicals leak into the ground where they are buried. These zombies can't talk, they smell awful and have no fashion sense!

A zombie can feed at any time of the night or day. But toxic zombies are good night hunters. They can sniff fresh blood a mile away. They can also hear you breathing from the other side of the street. Keep very quiet if there are any toxic zombies about!

A toxic zombie has no sense of feeling, and lots of energy. Even if a zombie's body is badly injured, it just keeps on attacking. They can walk for miles and miles, but they don't jump and they don't swim. When hunting for victims, they stumble about rather than tracking them down. Luckily, a zombie only lives as long as it takes for its body to rot away.

ZOMBIE LANGUAGE

Toxic zombies don't talk.
They just moan.
Their moans start as
a rumble. They get louder
and louder as they move
into the attack.
Then they rush at you
with open jaws.

UUURRRRRGGGGGG!

This is one of the most terrifying sounds you will ever hear. The moan also tells other zombies that people are nearby.

VOODOO ZOMBIES

Imagine being given a drug that makes you look dead. When you wake up, you can see, hear, and feel pain. But you can't control your body. You've become a voodoo zombie!

Voodoo zombies appear in stories from the Caribbean, Central and South America and the southern United States.

Voodoo sorcerers called houngans feed their victims with zombie powder. The powder makes the victims appear dead for up to two days. The voodoo zombies know what is happening around them, but they can't react.

After the person is buried, the houngan digs them up. They feed the victim more powder to make them stay a zombie. Then the houngan uses the voodoo zombie as a slave.

BURIED ALIVE

There is a possible explanation for these stories about digging up zombies. In the past, doctors might have buried someone who was still alive (or in a coma), by mistake.

If grave robbers dug up their bodies to steal the jewelry that was buried with them, the people seemed to come back to life. But they were really just waking up!

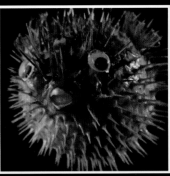

ZOMBIE DRUGS

Zombie powder can be used to shut down a victim's brain. The powder can be made from poisons taken from animals such as the spiky puffer fish (above), the hyla tree frog, or the cane toad.

Other voodoo zombie stories tell of people being forced to drink soup made from the leaves of the datura tree. The leaves contain a strong drug that is said to turn people into robots.

DEALING WITH ZOMBIES

EVERY ZOMBIE FOR ITSELF

Sometimes just a few zombies attack. But as people are bitten they turn into zombies as well. The numbers grow bigger and bigger. Soon, thousands of zombies are on the attack, like a swarm of rats.

Luckily, zombies aren't smart enough to work as a team. If they were, we'd all be zombies!

ZOMBIE DO'S AND DONT'S

You're alone in a dark, spooky house, miles from the nearest town. Outside zombies are gathering. Let's hope you packed well....

Here are some tips for staying alive if a gang of zombies are marching toward your house:

- Block off all doors and windows.
- Stay inside if you can and wait to be rescued.
- Gather food, water, torches, weapons and an emergency radio.
- Wear earplugs to cut out annoying zombie moans.
- Wear tight clothes so there is nothing for zombies to grab onto.
- Don't let zombies trap you in a corner.

If in doubt, run for it! You can move faster than a zombie. Make as little noise as possible and avoid open areas where you can be easily spotted!

DESTROYING ZOMBIES

Want to kill a zombie? Silver bullets won't work. Forget magic potions, spells or holy objects, such as crosses. In fact, there's only one way to kill a zombie—chop off its head!

A zombie's skull is rock-hard. It's much easier to chop it off with an axe or a sword, than to crush it with a hammer or a sledgehammer.

Power tools might seem like a good idea. But chainsaws are heavy and you may chop off bits of yourself by accident.

When tracking zombies, watch for freshly eaten bodies. Hunting zombies takes a lot of guts. Work in teams and whatever weapon you use, don't let zombies get close enough to bite you.

Zombies are slow. So it is always better to run than stand and fight.

ZOMBIE HUNTING

Running zombies over with a car works well. But you have to make sure you squash the zombie's head to kill it. Fire is no good because toxic zombies have no fear of fire. If they catch fire, they won't even notice it. A burning zombie becomes a living torch. It will set light to everything it touches, including you!

VIKING DRAUGR

The word zombie has been around for about 200 years. It comes from the African word "nzambi," which means the soul of a dead person. But some zombie tales are thousands of years old.

GRETTIR'S SAGA

"Grettir took all the treasure... but as he was making his way through the tomb he was grabbed by someone... they had a fierce struggle for a long time... but in the end the draugr fell backwards, and there was a great crash..."

This Viking story is over a 1,000 years old. It tells how a Viking grave robber was attacked by a draugr, who wanted to hold onto its treasure!

BLACK AS DEATH

A draugr was said to be "black as death." In some stories, a person killed by a draugr also turned black and became a zombie.

Draugr were really strong. One story tells of a victim left "with his neck broken and every bone in his body crushed." Some could change into a cat that sat on a sleeping person's chest so they suffocated.

When the body of a Viking warrior was placed in its tomb, it came alive again. These Viking zombies were called draugr. Some draugr attacked the living. Other draugr stayed in their tombs, guarding their treasures.

A draugr had superhuman strength. Only a powerful hero could defeat it. Like a toxic zombie, a draugr was killed by cutting off its head.

In some legends the hero had to leap between the head and the body before the two parts hit the ground! The draugr's body was then burnt. The ashes were buried in a remote spot or thrown into the sea.

GOLEMS

Would you like a trained zombie to protect you from attack or do boring jobs around the house? Magicians in the Middle Ages did! They created zombie slaves from clay and mud.

In Jewish stories, brainless zombies were called golems. Jewish holy men called rabbis created them.

The golem was brought to life using the holy word "Emet" which means "truth." This was written on the golem's forehead, or on a clay tablet put under its tongue. Golems could not speak or disobey their master.

In some stories the golem grew bigger and bigger. To stop the golem from hurting its friends as well as its enemies, the rabbi turned it back into dust by rubbing out the "E" of Emet. This spells "Met," which means "death" in Hebrew, the Jewish language.

THE LEGEND OF THE GOLEM OF PRAGUE

In the 16th century a rabbi called the Maharal of Prague created a golem. He wanted to defend the Jewish people in Prague from attacks. The golem was made of clay from the banks of the Vltava or Moldau river.

As the golem grew bigger and bigger, it started killing people. The city council promised the rabbi that the violence against the Jews would stop. So the rabbi turned the golem back into dust.

THE THINKING ZOMBIE

In the movie *The Fellowship of the Ring* (2001), the character of Lurtz is based on the golem legend.

Lurtz is a gruesome monster made from mud. He is brought to life by the evil sorcerer Saruman. Lurtz is different because he has a brain. He is a skilful fighter who leads an army of monsters. Lurtz is finally killed by having his head cut off— a classic zombie death!

REVENANTS

Are you good? In the Middle Ages, people believed that anyone who had led a wicked life would rise from their grave to haunt the living.

In the Middle Ages, zombies were called revenants. They were blamed for spreading disease.

In some countries, people tied up the arms and legs of a dead body to stop it becoming a revenant. Sometimes the mouth was sewn up.

In some legends, a powerful wizard brings the body of a dead hero to life to carry out a dangerous mission. This revenant would be just as clever as he was in life. But he would be controlled by the wizard.

THE LIVING DEAD

"The zombies appeared at evening, carrying on their shoulders the wooden coffins in which they had been buried... The villagers became sick and started dying. The bodies of the zombies were dug up... the heads cut off... this put an end to the spread of the sickness."

An account of the living dead, written by the Abbot of Burton around 1090 CE.

SKELETON ZOMBIES

In the ancient Greek story of Jason and the Argonauts, Jason and his men battle with zombie skeleton warriors. In one version of the story, Jason jumps into the sea. The skeletons follow but sink to the bottom!

This trick works on toxic zombies, too. If you swim across a lake, a toxic zombie will follow you, but it will soon sink to the bottom.

MUMMIES

A mummy walks towards its victims, its arms outstretched. Its ancient, crumbling body held together by bandages. Run for your life!

In the movie, *The Mummy* (1999) the ancient Egyptian priest Imhotep falls in love with the king's wife. Imhotep is buried alive for 3,000 years as a punishment. A group of archaeologists accidentally bring Imhotep's mummy back to life. The mummy goes on a killing spree. He uses his victims' bodies to rebuild his own rotting body.

Mummy stories may come from an ancient Egyptian myth. The god Osiris was killed by his brother Seth. His body was cut up by Seth and the pieces were scattered across Egypt. However, Osiris's wife, Isis tied the bloody bits together with bandages, and Osiris came back to life.

In the past, people thought mummies were magical. Many mummies were the dead bodies of ancient kings and queens. King Charles II rubbed ground-up mummy on his skin so that the "ancient greatness" would rub off on him!

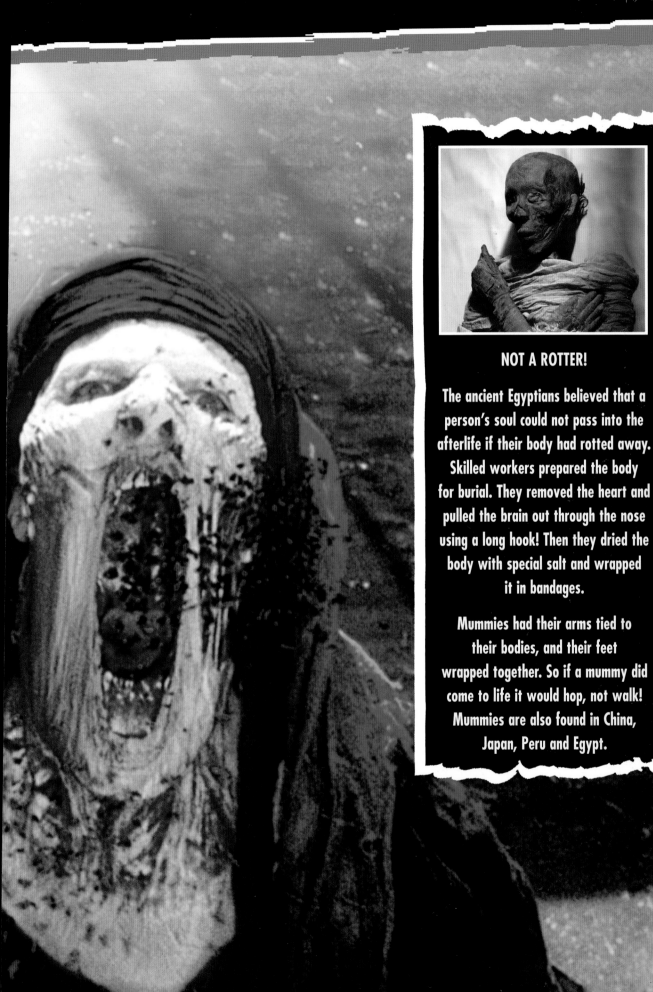

NOT A ROTTER!

The ancient Egyptians believed that a person's soul could not pass into the afterlife if their body had rotted away. Skilled workers prepared the body for burial. They removed the heart and pulled the brain out through the nose using a long hook! Then they dried the body with special salt and wrapped it in bandages.

Mummies had their arms tied to their bodies, and their feet wrapped together. So if a mummy did come to life it would hop, not walk! Mummies are also found in China, Japan, Peru and Egypt.

CHINESE HOPPING CORPSES

China has its very own zombie, the hopping corpse. This zombie will stop at nothing until it has chomped on your neck. Some will choke you while you sleep. Sweet dreams!

Jiangshi, or "stiff corpses," feed on people to take their life force. But why do they hop? When a person dies, their body goes all stiff. This is called rigor mortis. These zombies stay a bit stiff, so they can only hop!

Hopping corpses are very easy to spot. They usually wear burial clothes from the time of the Chinese Qing rulers (1644-1911). These clothes went out of fashion hundreds of years ago.

Some have black tongues that hang down to their chest. Others have eyeballs that hang from their sockets.

And they stink! Some hopping corpses smell so bad a single sniff will knock you out!

MOON ENERGY

Hopping corpses come to life using energy from the moon.

These zombies first appear in a myth called *The Corpses who Travel a Thousand Miles.* In this story, priests use magic spells to move corpses over long distances. They get them to hop back to their hometown for a proper burial.

HOPPING CORPSE PROTECTION ADVICE

- Don't breathe. The corpses hunt the living by smelling their breath.

- Piles of sticky rice stop hopping corpses moving.

- Burn the corpse to ashes, coffin and all.

- Some priests suggest nailing a piece of wood, about 5 inches high, across the bottom of your front door. Perhaps this stops zombies hopping into your house!

GHOULS

These thin-faced zombies with bulging, yellow eyes hang about in Arabian cemeteries. They carry sleepy travelers into the desert, then tear them apart with their large claws and teeth!

A ghoul has a huge mouth that is lined with rows of tiny razor-sharp teeth. It has long arms and short legs. Don't look at it too hard because it often appears naked. A toxic zombie only eats living people. But a ghoul loves human flesh so much it eats dead bodies too.

A ghoul's home is usually an underground tomb or crypt. The sun's rays make it weak, so it only goes looking for meat at night. It sees well at night, and can smell human flesh (alive or dead) up to a mile away.

THE BOGEYMAN

In Europe and North America there is a famous ghoul known as "the bogeyman." It enjoys hiding under beds or in closets in the dark. It waits until you are asleep then leaps out on you.

However, it only does this to scare you and is not that dangerous. The name bogeyman may come from the words "boggy man." Ancient bodies buried in peat bogs on moors were called "bog men." In the past, people were afraid that the bog men would come walking off the moors, like zombies!

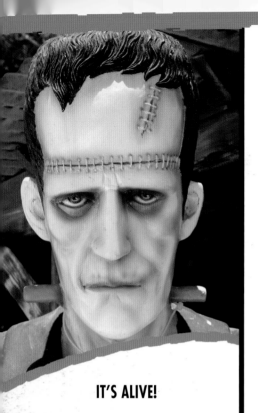

FRANKENSTEIN

Agiant man walks stiffly towards you. Ugly, square face. Bolts through the neck. Stitches all over his body. Uh-oh! It's Frankenstein's monster.

The author Mary Shelley created one of the most famous zombie-like monsters of all time in her book *Frankenstein* (1818).

Scientist Victor Frankenstein creates a monster in his laboratory from the body parts of several dead people. He sews the body bits together and uses electricity to bring the monster to life.

However, the monster is not a mindless zombie. He is clever, and knows how he was created. He feels emotions and pain.

After killing Frankenstein's brother, the monster hides in the mountains. He gets lonely, and asks Frankenstein to create a female monster to be his wife. Frankenstein does this, but then changes his mind. He destroys the female monster. This makes the monster so angry he kills Victor's father and wife.

IT'S ALIVE!

"It was on a dreary night of November... I collected the instruments of life around me, that I might infuse a spark of being into the lifeless thing... It was already one in the morning... and my candle was nearly burnt out, when... I saw the dull yellow eye of the creature open; it breathed hard, and moved its limbs."

From *Frankenstein* (1818) by Mary Shelley.

ON THE SCREEN

Zombies are everywhere! From the TV show *Buffy the Vampire Slayer*, to the walking dead that terrorize London in *Shaun of the Dead*.

Shaun has a dead-end job and his life is going nowhere. But then the flesh-hungry, living-dead start to appear in London. Shaun is forced to become a modern-day hero to save his girlfriend, his best friends, and his mom!

In the first movie to use the word "zombie," *White Zombie* (1932), a factory owner uses walking corpses as slaves.

Night of the Living Dead (1968), was the first movie to show the toxic zombies we know today. The zombies were brought to life by radiation from a space rocket.

Since then, zombies have appeared in countless movies. Special effects are used to show their rotting bodies and bloody attacks on humans.

ZOMBIE INVASIONS

Movies give all sorts of reasons for zombie outbreaks. In *Plan 9 from Outer Space* (1959), aliens bring dead humans back to life. They plan to use this army of zombies to take over the world.

A common movie plot is a plague that turns people into zombies. A small group of survivors have to find a way to survive and stop the plague.

COMPUTER ZOMBIES

Many computer games feature zombies as enemies. In the game *Zombies Ate My Neighbors*, the object of the game is to save your neighbors from being munched on by zombies. In the game *Resident Evil*, scientists turn into zombies after a virus escapes from a secret laboratory. *Resident Evil* has also been made into three movies.

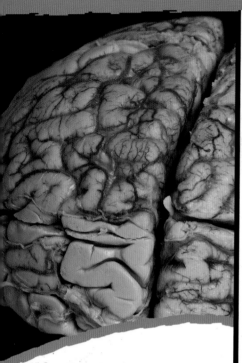

DO ZOMBIES EXIST?

In 1937, people in a village in Haiti in the Carribean reported that they had seen a woman called Felicia Felix-Mentor wandering around the village. She had been dead and buried for 30 years!

In 1980, a man appeared in a village in Haiti. He said he was Clairvius Narcisse, who had died in 1962. Narcisse said that poisons had made him seem dead. He had even seen the doctor cover his face with a sheet. Narcisse claimed that a sorcerer had brought him back to life and made him into a zombie.

Could these stories be true? Maybe. We know about some powerful poisons that can make a person look dead for several days. The victim continues to see and hear but can't move. Perhaps other poisons exist that can make someone seem dead, for years!

Still, strange poisons do not explain where crazy, brain-eating zombies come from!

TALL TALES?

Where do zombie stories come from?

The idea that zombies eat human brains may have come from cannibals in the South Pacific. They ate the brains of their enemies in order to gain extra powers.

Also, in the past, people were accidentally buried alive. This may be why people think it is possible for the dead to rise again!

GLOSSARY

Afterlife Where you go after you die.

Aristocrat A rich noble.

Berserkers Viking warriors who worked themselves into a violent frenzy before battle.

Bloodsucker An animal that sucks blood from other animals for food.

Bog men Dead bodies that are thousands of years old. They have been preserved in marshy ground.

Coffin A box in which a corpse is buried.

Coma Being deeply unconscious for a long time. A coma can be caused by an injury, an illness, or drugs.

Corpse A dead body.

Crowbar An iron bar with a flat end.

Crucifix A Christian symbol in the shape of a cross, said to scare off vampires.

Demon An evil spirit or monster.

Dhampir A half-human vampire that can find and kill their vampire relatives.

Executed To be killed as a punishment.

Garlic A bulb-like plant. It is thought to protect against vampires.

Golem A brainless zombie slave from Jewish stories. Golems were created by Jewish holy men, called rabbis. They were made from clay and mud. Having a golem slave was a sign of great holiness and wisdom.

Horde A large group of people.

Houngan A voodoo priest, usually from Haiti. Houngans can turn people into zombies.

Hypnosis When someone's words or actions make you fall into a sleep-like state in which you follow their commands.

Impale To kill someone on a sharp stake.

Legend A story about the past, often about supernatural events.

Mallet A hammer with a large wooden head.

Medieval A period in history from about 1000–1453.

Monastery A building where monks live.

Musket A long, old-fashioned gun.

Pentagram A five-pointed star that can be drawn in a continuous line and thought to be magical.

Pitchfork A long-handled tool with thin prongs. It is used for lifting and moving hay or straw.

Radiation Energy that is transmitted in waves or particles. Radiation can take the form of electromagnetic waves, such as heat, light, X-rays, or gamma rays.

Reflection An image that is shown back, usually in a mirror.

Revenants Zombies from the Middle Ages in Europe. It was thought that they were people who had been wicked in their lives.

Saga An ancient Viking story, often about heroes.

Shape-shifters People who can turn themselves into an animal. Often a sorcerer.

Sorcerer Someone who practises magic.

Stake A wooden stick with a sharp point. Used to kill vampires.

Superhuman Having incredible powers or strength, much greater than ordinary humans.

Supernatural Mysterious forces that cannot be explained by science or nature.

Tattoo A colored ink pattern on the skin made by pricking with a fine needle.

Telegraph A machine that sends messages along an electrical wire.

Transform To change from one thing into another. Vampires can transform into other animals such as bats.

Transylvania A part of Romania and the legendary home of Dracula.

Vampire A supernatural creature that feeds on the blood of human victims.

Vikings People from Norway, Denmark and Sweden who lived about 1,000 years ago. The Vikings were bloodthirsty warriors who explored Europe, Greenland and parts of North America by sea and land.

Voodoo A religion that began in West Africa. Today, it is mainly practised in Haiti in the Caribbean. Voodoo followers believe they can contact their dead ancestors while they are in a trance.

Were-creatures Humans that turn into animals, often predators (hunting animals), such as leopards, tigers, or wolves.

Werewolf A man or woman that turns into a wolf when there is a full moon.

Wolfsbane A plant that is said to protect against werewolves. It is very poisonous and can be deadly.